D1060815

Alex and Max

Mary Elizabeth Salzmann

Consulting Editor, Diane Craig, M.A./Reading Specialist

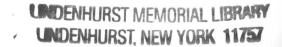

LINDENHURST MEMORIAL LIBRARY
LINDENHURST, NEW YORK 11757

Published by ABDO Publishing Company, 4940 Viking Drive, Edina, Minnesota 55435.

Copyright © 2005 by Abdo Consulting Group, Inc. International copyrights reserved in all countries. No part of this book may be reproduced in any form without written permission from the publisher. SandCastle™ is a trademark and logo of ABDO Publishing Company.

Printed in the United States.

Credits
Edited by: Pam Price
Curriculum Coordinator: Nancy Tuminelly
Cover and Interior Design and Production: Mighty Media
Child Photography: Steven Wewerka, Wewerka Photography
Photo Credits: AbleStock, Comstock, Corbis Images

Library of Congress Cataloging-in-Publication Data

Salzmann, Mary Elizabeth, 1968-
    Alex and Max / Mary Elizabeth Salzmann.
        p. cm. -- (First sounds)
    Includes index.
    ISBN 1-59679-122-5 (hardcover)
    ISBN 1-59679-123-3 (paperback)
    1. English language--Vowels--Juvenile literature. I. Title. II. Series.

PE1157.S25 2005
428.1'3--dc22
                                                                2004058973

SandCastle™ books are created by a professional team of educators, reading specialists, and content developers around five essential components that include phonemic awareness, phonics, vocabulary, text comprehension, and fluency. All books are written, reviewed, and leveled for guided reading, early intervention reading, and Accelerated Reader® programs and designed for use in shared, guided, and independent reading and writing activities to support a balanced approach to literacy instruction.

Let Us Know

After reading the book, SandCastle would like you to tell us your stories about reading. What is your favorite page? Was there something hard that you needed help with? Share the ups and downs of learning to read. We want to hear from you! To get posted on the ABDO Publishing Company Web site, send us e-mail at:

sandcastle@abdopub.com

SandCastle Level: Emerging

ABCDEFGH

IJKLMNOPQ

RSTUVWXYZ

abcdefgh

ijklmnopq

rstuvwxyz

Alex

Max

box

fox

mixer

X-ray

sax

Here is the .

Here is the .

Here is the .

Here is the .

Here is the .

16

Alex likes the sax.

Max likes the box.

The sax is in the box.

Which of these pictures have an x?

More words that have an x

exit

fax

fix

ox

six

tax

taxi

wax

About SandCastle™

A professional team of educators, reading specialists, and content developers created the SandCastle™ series to support young readers as they develop reading skills and strategies and increase their general knowledge. The SandCastle™ series has four levels that correspond to early literacy development in young children. The levels are provided to help teachers and parents select the appropriate books for young readers.

Emerging Readers
(no flags)

Beginning Readers
(1 flag)

Transitional Readers
(2 flags)

Fluent Readers
(3 flags)

These levels are meant only as a guide. All levels are subject to change.

ABDO
Publishing Company

To see a complete list of SandCastle™ books and other nonfiction titles from ABDO Publishing Company, visit www.abdopub.com or contact us at:
4940 Viking Drive, Edina, Minnesota 55435 • 1-800-800-1312 • fax: 1-952-831-1632